I0410235

Tithes: "Navigating Uncharted Waters:

Subtitle: A Guide to Avoiding Errors as a Left Field Investor"

By Jessica M.Brown

Copyright 2023, by Jessica M.Brown

All rights reserved. No part of this book may be reproduced in any form or by electronic or mechanical means, including information storage and retrieval systems, without permission from the publisher, except by a reviewer who may quote a brief passage in a review.

Table of Contents:

Chapter 12: Building Your Left Field Investment Plan

Chapter 1: Introduction

Left field investing refers to a unique and unconventional approach to allocating capital. Unlike traditional investment strategies that focus on stocks, bonds, and real estate, left field investing involves seeking opportunities in non-traditional and often overlooked asset classes. It's about thinking outside the box and exploring uncharted territories in pursuit of potentially higher returns.

The allure of left field investing lies in the potential for diversification and the pursuit of uncorrelated returns. By venturing into unconventional assets like rare collectibles, cryptocurrencies, startups, or even exotic commodities, investors can reduce their exposure to traditional market fluctuations. Additionally, these investments can provide a sense of excitement and the prospect of significant upside, appealing to risk-tolerant individuals. However, left field investing comes with its share of challenges and risks. Due diligence becomes more complex when dealing with less regulated or understood assets. Liquidity can be an issue, making it challenging to buy or sell these investments quickly. Moreover, the lack of historical data and market volatility can lead to higher uncertainty and potential losses. It's vital for left field investors to carefully assess their risk tolerance and thoroughly research any unconventional opportunities they pursue to mitigate these risks.

One of the primary reasons investors turn to left field investments is diversification. These assets often have low correlation with traditional markets, which means they may perform well when stocks or bonds are struggling. This diversification can help protect a portfolio during market downturns and enhance overall risk-adjusted returns.

Unconventional investments are often associated with innovation and emerging trends. Investing in startups, disruptive technologies, or niche markets can provide the opportunity to be part of groundbreaking developments. While these investments can be risky, they may also offer substantial growth potential if they succeed. Valuing unconventional assets can be challenging. Unlike publicly traded stocks with transparent pricing, the value of unique collectibles, private equity, or early-stage startups can be subjective and vary widely. Investors need to conduct thorough due diligence, understand the factors that drive value, and be cautious about overpaying for assets.

Many left field investments are illiquid, meaning they cannot be quickly converted into cash. This lack of liquidity can tie up capital for extended periods, making it crucial for investors to have a long-term perspective and a financial cushion to cover unexpected expenses.

Certain left field investments, like cryptocurrencies or alternative assets, may operate in regulatory gray areas or be subject to evolving regulations. Investors need to stay informed about legal and compliance requirements to avoid potential legal issues or unexpected changes in the investment landscape. While left field investments can be appealing, they should typically represent a smaller portion of an overall investment portfolio due to their higher risk profile. Diversification across various asset classes, including traditional ones, remains essential for managing risk effectively.

Left field investing offers the potential for diversification, innovation, and unique opportunities but comes with increased challenges and risks. It's essential for investors to strike a balance between conventional and unconventional assets, conduct thorough research, and align their investment choices with their risk tolerance and long-term financial goals.

Chapter 2: Research and Due Diligence

Thorough research is paramount in the world of investments, especially when identifying left-field opportunities and evaluating unique assets. It serves as the compass guiding investors towards informed decisions.

Firstly, comprehensive research helps mitigate risks. By delving deep into market trends, financial statements, and historical data, investors can spot potential pitfalls and avoid costly mistakes.

Secondly, it's crucial for identifying left-field opportunities. These are unconventional investments that often yield high returns. Thorough research uncovers these hidden gems, allowing investors to capitalize on them before they become mainstream.

Lastly, evaluating unique assets, such as cryptocurrencies or startups, demands meticulous research. Understanding the technology, team, and market dynamics is essential to gauge their potential and assess associated risks.

Thorough research isn't just a tool; it's the bedrock of successful investing. It empowers investors to navigate the complex financial landscape, unearth unconventional opportunities, and make sound decisions regarding unique assets.

Risk Mitigation: Thorough research provides a comprehensive understanding of the risks associated with an investment. It involves studying market conditions, analyzing historical performance, and assessing potential external factors that could impact the investment. This knowledge allows investors to make informed decisions and implement risk management strategies.

Identifying Left-Field Opportunities: Left-field opportunities are those that are not immediately apparent or popular among mainstream investors. Research involves staying ahead of the curve, tracking emerging trends, and exploring niche markets. It requires a keen eye for spotting opportunities that others may overlook, ultimately leading to the potential for higher returns.

Evaluating Unique Investment Assets: Unique assets can range from rare collectibles to innovative technologies. Research in this context involves understanding the intrinsic value, potential growth, and liquidity of these assets. For instance, when considering a cryptocurrency investment, one must delve into the underlying blockchain technology, assess the project's community and development team, and stay updated on regulatory developments.

In today's dynamic investment landscape, the importance of thorough research cannot be overstated. It empowers investors to make well-informed decisions, seize unconventional opportunities, and navigate the complexities of unique assets, ultimately increasing the likelihood of achieving their financial goals.

Chapter 3: Risk Assessment and Tolerance

Assessing Your Risk Tolerance: Evaluating your risk tolerance is a crucial step in financial planning. It involves understanding your ability and willingness to withstand investment fluctuations. Factors like financial goals, age, and personal temperament play a role. A high risk tolerance may lead to more aggressive investments, potentially yielding higher returns but with increased volatility. Conversely, a low risk tolerance may result in more conservative choices, emphasizing stability over growth. Striking the right balance aligns your investments with your comfort level and objectives.

Understanding the Volatility of Unconventional Assets:

Unconventional assets, such as cryptocurrencies, startups, and alternative investments, often exhibit greater price volatility compared to traditional assets like stocks and bonds. It's vital to comprehend this volatility before investing. Research and education are key; assess factors like market sentiment, technological developments, and regulatory changes. Diversification across asset classes can help mitigate risks associated with unconventional assets, spreading exposure across various investment types.

Balancing Risk:

Achieving a balanced investment portfolio is a cornerstone of risk management. Diversification, spreading investments across different assets and sectors, helps reduce overall risk. The goal is to create a portfolio that aligns with your risk tolerance and financial goals. Regularly reviewing and rebalancing your investments ensures that your risk remains in line with your objectives as market conditions change. Moreover, seeking professional financial advice can provide valuable insights into optimizing your risk-reward profile for long-term financial success.

Risk tolerance is not static; it can change over time due to factors like financial circumstances, life events, and evolving goals.

- To assess your risk tolerance, consider your investment horizon;

longer timelines often allow for higher risk tolerance as you can weather short-term fluctuations.

- Consult with a financial advisor or use risk tolerance questionnaires to gauge your comfort level with potential losses and gains.

Understanding the Volatility of Unconventional Assets:

- Unconventional assets often lack the historical data and regulatory oversight seen in traditional markets, making them riskier.

- Stay informed about the latest news and trends in the unconventional asset you're interested in; it can greatly affect their value.
- Allocate only a portion of your portfolio to unconventional assets, reducing exposure and potential losses.

Balancing Risk:

- The goal of balancing risk is to create a portfolio that maximizes returns while minimizing the chances of significant losses.

- Consider your financial goals when deciding how much risk to take on; short-term goals might require more conservative strategies.
- Regularly review your portfolio to ensure it aligns with your risk tolerance and adjust as needed to maintain balance.

Remember that risk is inherent in investing, but a well-thought-out approach can help you manage and potentially benefit from it. Always consider your unique financial situation

and seek professional advice when
necessary.

Chapter 4: Diversification Strategies

The Role of Diversification in Left Field Investing:

Diversification plays a crucial role in left field investing by spreading risk across various unconventional or non-traditional investments. It helps mitigate the higher inherent risk associated with these unique opportunities, allowing investors to benefit from potential gains while reducing the impact of potential losses.

Building a diverse portfolio involves allocating investments across different asset classes, geographic regions, industries, and asset types. This strategy helps manage risk and maximize potential returns. Regular rebalancing and staying informed are key components of successful portfolio diversification.

Avoiding Overconcentration: Overconcentration occurs when a substantial portion of your portfolio is invested in a single asset, sector, or asset class. To avoid this risk, set allocation limits, regularly monitor your portfolio, assess specific risks, stay informed, and consider seeking professional advice. Overconcentration is crucial for maintaining a well-balanced and risk-managed investment portfolio. In left field investing, which often involves unconventional or high-risk opportunities, diversification serves as a safety net. It involves spreading your investment capital across a variety of assets, not solely focused on left field opportunities. This strategy helps reduce the impact of potential losses from risky ventures. By diversifying, you balance the risk of left field investments with more stable assets, ultimately aiming for a smoother and potentially more profitable investment journey.

Building a diverse portfolio is a deliberate strategy to enhance your investment prospects. It entails:

Asset Allocation: Divide your investments among different asset classes, such as stocks, bonds, real estate, and alternative investments. Each asset class has its own risk and return profile.

Geographic Diversification: Invest in assets from various regions or countries. This approach guards against localized economic downturns or geopolitical risks.

Industry and Sector Diversification: Within stocks, diversify across various industries and sectors. Different sectors perform differently during economic cycles, reducing sector-specific risks.

Asset Types: Consider a mix of assets like growth stocks, value stocks, government bonds, corporate bonds, and commodities. Each type can react differently to market conditions.

Rebalancing: Periodically review and adjust your portfolio. Sell assets that have performed well and buy assets that have underperformed to maintain your desired asset allocation.

Avoiding Overconcentration: Overconcentration, or putting too much of your portfolio into a single investment, is a risk to be avoided. Here's how:

Set Allocation Limits: Define a maximum percentage of your portfolio for any one asset or sector. Stick to these limits to prevent overexposure.

Regular Monitoring: Keep a close eye on your investments. If one asset becomes a disproportionately large part of your portfolio due to substantial gains, consider rebalancing to maintain diversification.

Risk Assessment: Evaluate the specific risks associated with each investment. Diversify away from assets with correlated high risks.

Stay Informed: Stay up-to-date on market trends and economic developments. If a particular asset class or sector appears overvalued or risky, consider reducing your exposure.

Professional Guidance: Seek advice from financial experts to ensure your portfolio remains diversified and aligned with your financial goals. They can provide insights and strategies to avoid overconcentration.

Strategic asset allocation, and vigilant risk management are vital in both conventional and left field investing. These principles help investors navigate uncertain terrain, manage risk, and maximize their chances of achieving their financial objectives while exploring unconventional investment opportunities.Avoiding overconcentration and employing a thoughtful diversification strategy are key elements of a successful investment approach.

Chapter 5: Seeking Expert Advice

Consulting Specialists and Experts:

Consulting specialists and experts is a fundamental aspect of problem-solving and decision-making in various fields. These individuals possess in-depth knowledge and experience, offering invaluable insights and guidance. By seeking their advice, you can make informed choices, avoid common pitfalls, and achieve better outcomes.Consulting specialists and experts is not just about seeking advice; it's about tapping into a wealth of knowledge and experience that can save you time, resources, and potential mistakes. Specialists are often at the forefront of their respective fields, staying up-to-date with the latest trends and innovations. When you consult them, you gain access to cutting-edge insights that can be applied to your projects or decisions. Additionally, experts can provide a fresh perspective, challenging your assumptions and leading to creative problem-solving. Whether it's in medicine, technology, finance, or any other domain, consulting specialists can be the key to unlocking success.

The Value of Mentorship:

Mentorship plays a pivotal role in personal and professional growth. Having a mentor provides you with a seasoned guide who can offer advice, share wisdom, and help you navigate challenges. Mentorship fosters skill development, confidence, and a broader perspective, ultimately propelling you towards success and self-improvement. Mentorship is a dynamic relationship that goes beyond mere guidance. A mentor serves as a role model, offering not only advice but also emotional support and encouragement. They can help you set and achieve meaningful goals, develop critical skills, and navigate the complexities of your chosen path. Through mentorship, you gain a personalized learning experience, tailored to your unique needs and aspirations. Moreover, mentors often have extensive networks, which can introduce you to valuable contacts and opportunities. Ultimately, mentorship is an investment in your personal and professional growth, and it's a two-way street where both mentor and mentee benefit

Building a Network in Your Chosen Field:

Networking is a crucial step in advancing your career or pursuing your passion. Building connections with like-minded individuals and professionals in your chosen field opens doors to opportunities, collaboration, and knowledge exchange. A strong network not only enhances your visibility but also enriches your expertise by exposing you to diverse perspectives and experiences.

Whether you're consulting specialists for expertise, seeking mentorship for guidance, or expanding your network in your chosen field, these endeavors are instrumental in personal and professional development, offering a pathway to success and growth.

Networking is about more than just collecting business cards or LinkedIn connections; it's about building meaningful relationships. Your network can include peers, colleagues, industry leaders, and potential collaborators. By actively participating in your field's community, attending conferences, joining professional organizations, and engaging in online forums, you create a web of connections that can provide you with support, advice, and opportunities. Networking is an ongoing process that can open doors to jobs, partnerships, and shared knowledge. It's a vital aspect of career development, and the strength of your network often correlates with your ability to achieve your goals. Consulting specialists and experts, seeking mentorship, and building a strong network are essential components of personal and professional growth. They can accelerate your learning, provide

valuable insights, and create a supportive
ecosystem that propels you toward
success in your chosen field. These
actions not only benefit you individually
but also contribute to the collective
knowledge and progress of your
profession.

Chapter 6: Staying Informed

In recent years, the world of investments has witnessed a dramatic shift towards unconventional opportunities. Traditional stocks and bonds are no longer the sole focus of investors. This evolution is driven by factors such as technological advancements, changing market dynamics, and the quest for higher returns. As a result, investors are exploring a diverse range of assets, including cryptocurrencies, NFTs, peer-to-peer lending, and more.The Rapidly Changing Landscape of Unconventional Investments:

In recent years, the realm of investments has undergone a seismic transformation, marked by a palpable shift toward unconventional opportunities. This evolution is propelled by a confluence of factors, including technological innovation, shifting market dynamics, and the ceaseless quest for higher returns. As a result, investors are increasingly diversifying their portfolios by exploring a wide spectrum of non-traditional assets. These encompass cryptocurrencies, non-fungible tokens (NFTs), peer-to-peer lending platforms, alternative energy ventures, and more

In this dynamic landscape, staying well-informed is paramount. Investors rely heavily on a multitude of information and news sources to make informed decisions. Traditional financial news outlets, social media platforms, and specialized investment websites provide real-time updates and expert analyses. However, the decentralized and sometimes speculative nature of unconventional investments demands careful discernment of information sources. Distinguishing between credible news and market noise is crucial to navigate this rapidly evolving field.In this dynamic landscape, the ability to access, analyze, and act upon timely information is paramount. Investors now find themselves relying heavily on a plethora of information and news sources to make well-informed decisions. Traditional financial news outlets continue to provide insights, but the rise of social media platforms and specialized investment websites has democratized access to real-time updates and expert analyses. Yet, with the decentralized and sometimes speculative nature of unconventional investments, there is an inherent need for discernment in choosing which sources to trust. Distinguishing between credible news and market noise becomes a vital skill in navigating this rapidly evolving field.

Engaging with like-minded individuals in forums and online communities has become an integral part of the investment process. These platforms offer valuable insights, shared experiences, and collaborative learning opportunities. From Reddit's WallStreetBets to cryptocurrency-focused subreddits and Discord groups, investors come together to discuss strategies, share tips, and exchange ideas. It's important to approach these communities with a critical mindset, as they can be both informative and risky due to the influence of market sentiment and hype.It serve as hubs where investors gather to discuss strategies, share personal experiences, and foster collaborative learning. For instance, platforms like Reddit host subreddits such as WallStreetBets, which gained notoriety for its influence on the GameStop stock saga. Similarly, cryptocurrency enthusiasts converge on various crypto-focused subreddits and

Discord groups. These communities can be wellsprings of valuable insights, but they should also be approached with caution. The influence of market sentiment and hype can be strong, potentially leading to impulsive investment decisions. In conclusion, the landscape of unconventional investments is continuously evolving, offering both unprecedented opportunities and inherent risks. To navigate this terrain successfully, investors must remain vigilant, staying well-informed through a variety of sources, and actively participating in relevant forums and communities. This dynamic environment requires adaptability, critical thinking, and a commitment to ongoing education to maximize the potential benefits while minimizing the associated risks.

Chapter 7: Long-Term Perspective

Left field investments, often unconventional or unorthodox in nature, demand a unique trait from investors: patience. Unlike traditional assets, these ventures may take longer to mature or realize returns. Whether it's a startup, a niche technology, or an emerging market, success often unfolds over years, not months. Embracing a patient approach allows investors to weather the uncertainties and volatility inherent in these opportunities, providing the time needed for them to potentially bear fruit.

In the world of left field investments, the allure of quick gains can be tempting. However, yielding to short-term thinking is often counterproductive. Investors must resist the urge to chase immediate profits, recognizing that the most promising ventures may require time to develop and gain traction. Short-termism can lead to impulsive decisions and missed opportunities for long-term growth. Instead, a focus on the bigger picture and the underlying fundamentals of the investment is essential.

Market fluctuations are an intrinsic part of any investment landscape, and left field investments are no exception. Prices can be highly volatile, testing the resolve of investors. To succeed in this arena, it's imperative to stay steady during market turbulence. Holding onto your investments through these fluctuations can be the key to realizing substantial gains in the end. Attempting to time the market or panic-selling during downturns often results in missed opportunities and losses. left field investments demand a distinct mindset, one characterized by patience, a long-term perspective, and the resilience to withstand market ups and downs. By avoiding short-term thinking and holding firm through fluctuations, investors can position themselves for the potential rewards these unconventional opportunities can offer over time.

Chapter 8: Risk Management Strategies

Risk management is essential in any financial endeavor. Here are three key strategies:

Setting Stop-Loss Orders: This strategy involves predefining a point at which you will sell an asset to limit potential losses. It helps protect your capital and ensures you exit a trade when it moves against your expectations. When setting a stop-loss order, you specify a price at which your asset will be automatically sold. This ensures that if the market moves against your position, you limit your potential losses. However, it's essential to strike a balance between setting a stop-loss too tight (risking premature exits) and too wide (exposing yourself

Establishing Exit Criteria: Beyond stop-loss orders, having clear exit criteria for your investments is crucial. These criteria could be based on profit targets, timeframes, or specific events. They help you maintain discipline and prevent emotional decision-making. Exit criteria go beyond just preventing losses; they also include taking profits. For instance, you might decide to exit a trade when you've achieved a certain percentage gain or when a stock reaches a specific price target. Having these criteria in place helps you stick to your trading plan and avoid impulsive decisions driven by emotions.

Hedging Against Unpredictable Outcomes: Hedging involves taking positions that offset potential losses in your primary investments. It's particularly useful in volatile markets. Common hedging tools include options, futures, and derivatives, which can help mitigate risks associated with unexpected market shifts.Hedging Against Unpredictable Outcomes: Hedging is akin to buying insurance for your investments. For example, if you hold a portfolio of stocks and are concerned about market downturns, you might purchase put options to protect against potential declines. While hedging comes at a cost, it can provide peace of mind and reduce overall portfolio risk

Risk management is an integral part of financial decision-making. These strategies, when used effectively, not only protect your investments but also contribute to a more structured and rational approach to trading and investing. Remember that the specific strategy you choose should align with your risk tolerance, investment goals, and market conditions.

Chapter 9: Tax Implications

Investors exploring unconventional assets, such as cryptocurrencies, art, or rare collectibles, should be mindful of unique tax implications. Unlike traditional investments, these assets often require specialized tax knowledge.

Navigating the complex tax landscape of unconventional assets can be daunting. Collaborating with experienced tax professionals is crucial. They can help you understand reporting requirements, deductions, and potential tax liabilities associated with your unique investments.

Tax-Efficient Strategies for Left Field Investors:

Left field investors can employ several tax-efficient strategies:

- Holding Period: Longer holding periods often qualify for lower capital gains tax rates. Consider a buy-and-hold strategy to reduce tax obligations.

- Tax-Advantaged Accounts: Utilize tax-advantaged accounts like IRAs or 401(k)s when possible. Some unconventional assets can be held within these accounts, providing tax advantages.
- Gifts and Inheritance: Gifting or inheriting unconventional assets may have tax advantages. Consult with a tax professional to understand the best approach.
- Tax-Loss Harvesting: Offset gains by strategically selling assets that have declined in value to minimize taxable income.
- Charitable Donations: Donating unconventional assets to charities can provide tax deductions while supporting a good cause.
- 1031 Exchanges: Explore 1031 exchanges for certain assets like real estate, which can defer capital gains taxes.

- Tax Credits: Investigate available tax credits related to renewable energy investments or other unconventional ventures.
- Valuation and Reporting: Determining the fair market value of unconventional assets can be challenging. Ensure accurate valuation and proper reporting to avoid IRS scrutiny.
- Self-Directed IRAs: Consider using a self-directed IRA to invest in unconventional assets like real estate, private equity, or certain cryptocurrencies. This allows for tax-advantaged growth within the IRA.
- Tax Deferral: Explore options for deferring taxes on capital gains.

Some investments, like Qualified Opportunity Zones (QOZs), offer tax deferral and potential reductions.

- State Taxes: Be aware that state tax laws may differ from federal tax laws. Investigate how your state taxes unconventional assets and plan accordingly.
- Tax Documentation: Maintain detailed records of transactions, purchases, and sales related to unconventional assets. Proper documentation is essential for accurate tax reporting.
- Tax Withholding: If you receive income from unconventional assets, consider whether tax withholding is required. Failure to withhold can lead to penalties.
- Tax-Advantaged Accounts for Education: Use 529 plans or Coverdell ESAs to save for

education expenses with potential tax benefits.

- Estate Planning: Develop an estate plan that addresses the transfer of unconventional assets to heirs. Estate taxes can significantly impact your legacy.
- Tax Efficient Trading: If you actively trade unconventional assets, employ tax-efficient trading strategies to minimize short-term capital gains.
- Tax Diversification: Diversify your investments across different asset classes to balance tax implications and risk.
- Foreign Asset Reporting: If you hold unconventional assets in foreign accounts, comply with Foreign Bank Account Reporting (FBAR) and Foreign Account Tax Compliance Act (FATCA) requirements.

- Tax Software and Tools: Utilize specialized tax software or tools designed for unconventional assets to simplify reporting and calculations.
- Stay Informed: Tax laws and regulations change over time. Stay informed about updates that may affect your unconventional asset investments.

successfully managing the tax considerations for unconventional assets requires a proactive approach. Keep up-to-date with tax laws, consult experts when needed, and implement strategies tailored to your specific investments to maximize tax efficiency.

Chapter 10: Emotional Discipline

Emotional decision-making can lead to impulsive choices with potentially negative consequences. To avoid this, start by recognizing your emotions and taking a step back to analyze the situation objectively. Consider the facts, weigh pros and cons, and consult trusted advisors when necessary. Setting clear goals and following a predetermined decision-making process can help you stay rational and minimize emotional influence on your choices.

Handling Fear of Missing Out (FOMO):

The fear of missing out (FOMO) can lead to poor decisions driven by social pressure or the desire to keep up with others. To manage FOMO, begin by acknowledging its existence and impact on your decisions. Practice mindfulness to stay present and content with your current choices. Prioritize your goals and values, and remind yourself that you can't do everything. Focus on what truly matters to you, and don't let external pressures dictate your decisions.

Cultivating Emotional Resilience:

Emotional resilience is the ability to bounce back from setbacks and maintain mental well-being. To cultivate it, start by developing self-awareness. Recognize your emotions, their triggers, and how they affect your thoughts and actions. Build a support network of friends, family, or a therapist who can provide guidance and understanding during tough times. Practice stress management techniques, such as mindfulness, exercise, and deep breathing, to better cope with adversity. Embrace change as an opportunity for growth, and maintain a positive outlook by focusing on solutions rather than dwelling on problems. Developing emotional resilience takes time and effort, but it can greatly enhance your ability. Cultivating emotional resilience involves ongoing efforts and a commitment to personal growth:

- Adaptability: Embrace change as a constant in life. Be flexible and open to new experiences and challenges. This adaptability can help you navigate unexpected situations with greater ease.
- Self-compassion: Treat yourself with kindness and understanding, especially during difficult times. Avoid self-criticism and negative

self-talk. Self-compassion can boost your emotional resilience by providing a supportive inner voice.

- Positive Relationships: Nurture healthy and supportive relationships with those around you. Having a strong social support system can significantly bolster your emotional resilience. Seek out friends and loved ones who provide encouragement and empathy.
- Problem-Solving Skills: Develop effective problem-solving skills to address issues constructively. Break problems into smaller, manageable steps and focus on solutions rather than dwelling on the difficulties.
- Emotional Regulation: Learn to manage your emotions effectively. Techniques like meditation, mindfulness, and deep breathing can help you stay calm and

composed during challenging situations.

- Seek Professional Help: If you find it difficult to manage your emotions or if you're facing overwhelming challenges, consider seeking the assistance of a mental health professional. They can provide guidance and tools to enhance your emotional resilience.
- Learn from Setbacks: Instead of viewing setbacks as failures, see them as opportunities for growth and learning. Reflect on what you can gain from these experiences and how they can make you stronger.
- Maintain Physical Health: Regular exercise, a balanced diet, and sufficient sleep contribute to emotional resilience by ensuring your body is better equipped to handle stress.

Remember that emotional resilience is a lifelong journey, and it's normal to have moments of vulnerability. By consistently practicing these strategies and prioritizing your mental well-being, you can build the inner strength needed to thrive in the face of life's challenges.

Chapter 11: Learning from Mistakes

Embracing Mistakes as Learning Opportunities, Mistakes are not setbacks but stepping stones on our journey of growth and improvement. By analyzing past errors and implementing changes based on experience, we can transform these missteps into valuable learning opportunities. To benefit from our mistakes, we must first understand their root causes. Reflecting on what went wrong, why it happened, and the consequences helps us gain insights into our actions and decisions. This self-awareness is essential for personal and professional development. Once we've identified the lessons from our mistakes, it's crucial to take concrete steps to implement changes. Adjusting our approach, refining strategies, and avoiding repeating the same errors is the practical application of our newfound knowledge. This proactive response turns failures into catalysts for improvement.

Embracing learning opportunities involves a two-step process: analyzing past errors to understand them better and implementing changes based on the lessons learned. This mindset not only fosters personal growth but also paves the way for success in future endeavors.

Chapter 12: Building Your Left Field Investment Plan

A personalized investment plan is the foundation of successful investing. Start by assessing your financial situation, risk tolerance, and investment goals. Tailor your plan to match your unique circumstances, whether it's for retirement, education, or wealth accumulation. Diversify your investments across asset classes like stocks, bonds, and real estate to manage risk effectively. Regularly review and adjust your plan as your circumstances change.

Setting Clear Goals and Milestones:

Setting clear investment goals and milestones is crucial for staying on track. Define specific, measurable objectives with timelines. Whether it's saving a certain amount for a down payment on a house or reaching a retirement nest egg, having clear goals provides direction and motivation for your investment journey.

Tracking and Reviewing Progress:

Consistently monitor your investments to ensure they align with your goals. Regularly review your portfolio's performance, assess your risk tolerance, and make adjustments as needed. Stay informed about market trends and economic developments to make informed decisions. Tracking progress helps you stay accountable and make necessary corrections along the way.

The Rewards and Challenges of Left Field Investing:

Left field investing, also known as contrarian investing, involves going against the crowd and taking unconventional positions. The potential rewards can be substantial, with opportunities to buy undervalued assets and profit when markets correct.

However, the challenges include heightened risk and the need for extensive research. Left field investors must possess a strong conviction in their strategies and be prepared for potential volatility. As a left field investor, your journey may be less traveled, but it can be rewarding. Be prepared for periods of uncertainty and skepticism from others. Stay committed to your research and analysis, and remember that unconventional investments may take time to bear fruit. Embrace the learning process and adapt your strategies as you gain experience. Successful investing, whether conventional or contrarian, requires patience, discipline, and continuous learning. Diversify your portfolio, manage risk, and stay focused on your long-term goals. Avoid emotional reactions to market fluctuations, as they can lead to poor decisions. Seek advice from trusted financial professionals when needed, and remember that investing is a journey that unfolds over time. Stay committed, and your efforts can lead to financial security and growth.

www.ingramcontent.com/pod-product-compliance
Lightning Source LLC
Chambersburg PA
CBHW062239290526
45794CB00006B/2350